SCHOLASTIC

SMART Board® Lessons:
Math Word Problems

Ready-to-Use, Motivating Lessons on CD to Help You Teach
Essential Problem-Solving Skills

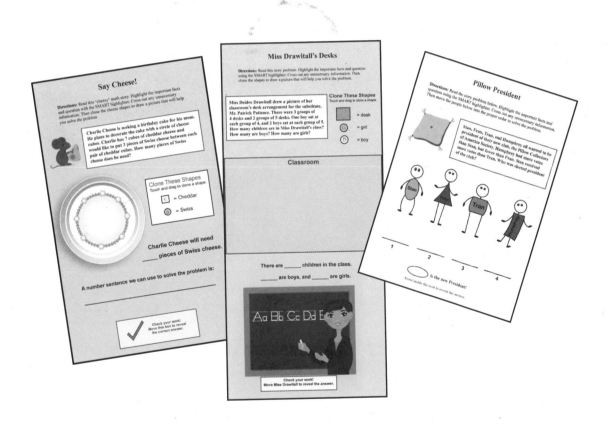

By Bob Krech, Diane Birrer, and Stephanie DiLorenzo

New York • Toronto • London • Auckland • Sydney
Mexico City • New Delhi • Hong Kong • Buenos Aires

Teaching Resources

Text © 2010 by Bob Krech

Illustrated by Kelly J. Brownlee

Edited by Maria L. Chang and Betsy Pringle

Designed by Rosanna Brockley

Design assistance by Ana-Maria Brujban and Shane Hartley

Cover design by Brian Larossa

Production by Jennifer Marx

SMARTBoard®Lessons: Math Word Problems is produced by **becker&mayer!**, Bellevue, WA 98004

ISBN-13: 978-0-545-14024-9

ISBN-10: 0-545-14024-2

08157

All rights reserved.

Printed, manufactured, and assembled in Hong Kong, China 12/09.

1 2 3 4 5 6 7 8 9 10   15 14 13 12 11 10

Table of Contents

Introduction

The National Council of Teachers of Mathematics made an important statement about problem solving in their *Principles and Standards for School Mathematics* (NCTM, 2000). They wrote: *"Problem solving should be the central focus of all mathematics instruction and an integral part of all mathematical activity."* In other words, problem solving is what math is all about.

SMART Board® Lessons: Math Word Problems is designed to help you increase your students' mathematical problem-solving abilities and, thus, their personal math power. By learning the Fantastic Five-Step Process and the Super 7 Strategies, students will acquire a set of tools they can use again and again to solve different types of word problems. These strategies will help them become efficient and accurate mathematical problem solvers. Combining these useful strategies with lessons created especially for the SMART Board results in a learning experience that is motivating, exciting, and successful. Here's how:

- The SMART Board offers instant lesson engagement. Whether you're teaching algebra, fractions, or problem solving, you will have students' immediate attention. Many of today's kids were computer literate before they started school. They're accustomed to games and gadgets that respond to the touch of a fingertip. A SMART Board grabs their attention in ways blackboards and handouts fail to do.

- Because it offers a large, interactive display and opportunities for collaborative learning, the SMART Board is a smart way to teach students 21st-century skills like working in teams, marking text electronically, synthesizing information, organizing data, interpreting visual aids, and evaluating Web sites. These skills are an increasingly important part of the standards in many states.

- The SMART Board is easy to use, even for technophobes. Using the board itself and the accompanying Notebook software is fairly intuitive. On the interactive whiteboard, you can do anything you can do on your computer screen—and then some. So, even if you are just learning the technology, you can pull off a fun, effective lesson. The lessons on this CD will make it easy.

Using the CD and Book

This book and CD will help you make the most of SMART technology within your math curriculum. The SMART Notebook pages on the CD are a perfect way to teach problem-solving skills because they allow you to model concepts and skills for the whole class. You can read and analyze word problems together, deciding which information is important and which is irrelevant. You can draw and move objects, highlight, underline, and write text right on the interactive whiteboard. And, best of all, you can save *everything* for later use or review. Distribute copies of the completed Notebook pages to students as reminders of learned strategies.

The CD features eight units that introduce the Fantastic Five-Step Process and Super 7 Strategies for solving word problems. Each unit is on the CD as a Notebook file with six interactive pages. These pages take advantage of the bells and whistles SMART technology has to offer without overwhelming the SMART Board novice. You'll find opportunities to use the SMART Board's pens, on-screen keyboard, cloning tools, drag-and-drop feature, and much more. Instructions for using each SMART tool are embedded in the lesson plans in this book.

Each unit on the CD is complete—you will not need to build onto or alter any of the pages in order to teach the lessons in this book. The first page in each unit introduces the problem-solving strategy, engages students' attention, and establishes what they already know. The next three pages contain word problems that challenge students to practice the particular strategy collaboratively. Also included in the unit are the assigned homework and the solution, which appears on a separate page. This allows you to preview the homework at the end of a lesson and use the solution page to review the assignment together as a class.

This book contains easy-to-use lessons that correspond to each CD unit. Lessons include step-by-step directions for teaching with each SMART Notebook page on the CD as well as reproducible practice sheets for students to try out the strategies independently. They also correlate with NCTM standards (see pages 6–7).

Tech Tips

Although the *SMART Board Lessons: Math Word Problems* CD was created using Notebook 10 software, you will be able to use the activities with older versions of the software. If you are still getting the hang of your SMART Board, be sure to look for the technology tips offered at various points throughout the book. Here is an overview of the main Notebook features you will be using.

 SMART Pens These are the black, red, green, and blue pens that come with your SMART Board. Use them to write directly on the screen in digital ink.

 Eraser Like its old-fashioned counterparts, this eraser removes unwanted writing. It will work on text and lines created with the SMART pens. It will not work on typed text or art objects.

 Screen Shade A teacher favorite, this tool allows you to cover part of a page while focusing attention on another part. Activate the shade by clicking on the Screen Shade icon on your toolbar. Deactivate it by clicking again. To gradually open a shade that covers your screen, use one of the circular buttons on the shade itself to drag the shade open.

Getting Started

- Before students arrive, have your SMART Board ready to go. Load the *SMART Board Lessons: Math Word Problems* CD onto your host computer and copy all the Notebook files onto your hard drive. This way, you can work off the local files when you're ready to teach a lesson.

- To get the most out of each Notebook page, maximize the window displaying the page. You can also go under View (in the pull-down menu on top of your screen) and click on either Full Screen or Zoom, which offers other page sizing options.

Meeting the NCTM Standards*

The lessons in this book and CD correlate with the following NCTM standards:

Number and Operations

- Students will understand numbers, ways of representing numbers, relationships among numbers, and number systems.
- Students will understand meanings of operations and how they relate to one another.
- Students will compute fluently and make reasonable estimates.

Algebra

- Students will understand patterns, relations, and functions.
- Students will represent and analyze mathematical situations and structures using algebraic symbols.
- Students will use mathematical models to represent and understand quantitative relationships.
- Students will analyze change in various contexts.

Geometry

- Students will use visualization, spatial reasoning, and geometric modeling to solve problems.

Measurement

- Students will understand measurable attributes of objects and the units, systems, and processes of measurement.

Problem Solving

- Students will build new mathematical knowledge through problem solving.
- Students will solve problems that arise in mathematics and in other contexts.
- Students will apply and adapt a variety of appropriate strategies to solve problems.
- Students will monitor and reflect on the process of mathematical problem solving.

Reasoning and Proof

- Students will recognize reasoning and proof as fundamental aspects of mathematics.

Communication

- Students will organize and consolidate their mathematical thinking through communication.
- Students will communicate their mathematical thinking coherently and clearly to peers, teachers, and others.
- Students will analyze and evaluate the mathematical thinking and strategies of others.
- Students will use the language of mathematics to express mathematical ideas precisely.

Connections

- Students will recognize and use connections among mathematical ideas.
- Students will understand how mathematical ideas interconnect and build on one another to produce a coherent whole.
- Students will recognize and apply mathematics in contexts outside of mathematics.

Representation

- Students will create and use representations to organize, record, and communicate mathematical ideas.
- Students will select, apply, and translate among mathematical representations to solve problems.
- Students will use representations to model and interpret physical, social, and mathematical phenomena.

* Source: *Principles and Standards for School Mathematics* (NCTM, 2000).

THE FANTASTIC FIVE-STEP PROCESS

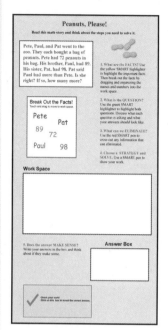

Word problems often intimidate students for several reasons. There may be a lot of information; the important facts are embedded in text; and, unlike a regular equation, it is not always clear to students exactly what they are supposed to do. No matter what type of problem students encounter, the Fantastic Five-Step Process will help them through it. Learning and using the five steps will help students organize their thinking—the key to effective problem solving.

GETTING READY

Before students arrive, have your SMART Board ready to go. Open the Fantastic Five-Step Process Notebook file. The first interactive page, *Peanuts, Please!*, will appear on your SMART Board. Make sure the Screen Shade tool is concealing the text in red on the right side of the page.

INTRODUCING THE CONCEPT

1. Display *Peanuts, Please!* on the SMART Board. Have students read the word problem silently. After sufficient time, invite a student volunteer to read the problem aloud to the class. Then tell students that together you will go through the steps of solving a word problem.

> Pete, Paul, and Pat went to the zoo. They each bought a bag of peanuts. Pete had 72 peanuts in his bag. His brother, Paul, had 89. His sister, Pat, had 98. Pat said Paul had more than Pete. Is she right? If so, how many more?

2. Ask students, "What do you think is the first step to solving a word problem?" Listen to a few responses, then slide down the Screen Shade tool to reveal **Step #1: What are the facts?** Ask, "What are the important facts that we need to know to solve this problem?" Invite a student to come to the board and use the yellow highlighter to highlight the important facts. Explain to students that these facts can be written in a more concise form. Have another student come to the board to "break out the facts" by dragging the names and their corresponding numbers into a list on the Work Space below.

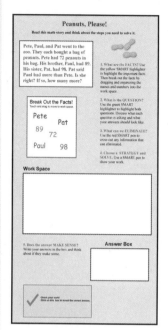

TECH TIP

To access a highlighter, have the student use a finger to tap on the SMART pens icon, then select the wide yellow line style. The student can now drag a finger over the desired text to highlight it.

3. Slide down the Screen Shade to reveal **Step #2: What is the question?** Ask, "What are we trying to find out? What question(s) do we need to answer?" Have a student come to the board and use the green highlighter to highlight the questions. Make sure students understand that in this particular problem there are two things we want to know: Was Pat right when she said Paul had more peanuts than Pete? If so, how many more peanuts does Paul have than Pete? Emphasize to students that they need to label their answer. For example, if the answer is 72, will it be 72 cats? 72 coins? 72 peanuts?

4. Next, slide down the Screen Shade to reveal **Step #3: What can we eliminate?** Explain to students that once we know what we are trying to find out, we can decide what is unimportant. We may need all the information, but often there is extra information that can be put aside or eliminated to help us focus on the facts. Ask a student to come to the board and draw a red line through any information that can be eliminated. In this problem, we can eliminate the fact that Pat had 98 peanuts. It's not needed to answer the question. We're left with

> Pete – 72
>
> Paul – 89

By comparing the numbers, we can answer the first part of the question. Pat was right. Paul has more peanuts than Pete.

5. Click or tap on the red button on the Screen Shade to remove it completely and reveal **Step #4: Choose a strategy and solve.** Ask, "Is there an action in the story, like something being taken away or shared, that will help us decide on an operation or a way to solve the problem?" Invite a student volunteer to come to the board and show his or her thinking on the Work Space. Since we are comparing two numbers in this problem, we have to find the difference. Usually the best way is to subtract or add up.

> $89 - 72 = 17$ OR $72 + 17 = 89$ OR $72 + 10 = 82 + 7 = 89$

We see that Paul had 17 more peanuts than Pete.

6. Scroll down below the Work Space to read **Step #5: Does the answer make sense?** Have the class reread the problem and look at the answer. Is it a reasonable answer given what we know? The answer makes sense for several reasons. For one, 17 is a lower number than the higher number we started with. If it were higher, that would indicate that something was wrong because the difference between two positive whole numbers cannot be higher than the highest number. Also, if we estimate by rounding, we see that Paul has about 90 peanuts and Pete has about 70. The difference between 90 and 70 is 20, and 17 is reasonably close to that.

7. To check the answer, click on the yellow box at the bottom of the page. The box will fade out to reveal the correct answer.

1. Display *Reviewing the Five-Step Process* on the SMART Board. Invite students to think about each step they used to solve the word problem they just completed. If necessary, guide them to recall each step in order. Click on the rectangles to reveal the steps.

2. Ask students: "How is this process helpful in solving a word problem? What does it do for us?" (*It helps us organize our thinking so we can decide on the best action for solving the problem.*)

3. Distribute photocopies of the *Fantastic Five-Step Process* worksheet (page 12) to students. Allow them to work in pairs and give them some time to solve the problems. Remind them to use the Fantastic Five-Step Process. When everyone has finished, display the Notebook page *Go Frogs!* on the SMART Board. Invite students to come to the board to work through the steps and demonstrate their understanding. Repeat the process with the *Fast Fliers!* Notebook page.

Answers:

Go Frogs! Smellbad Stadium

Fast Fliers! The Fling

TECH TIP

If highlighting or underline marks don't show up exactly where you want them, it's probably a sign that your SMART Board needs to be reoriented. Orienting ensures that your board is properly aligned. It is especially important to reorient if you are using a portable SMART Board unit. To orient, look at the Notebook software's startup menu.

EXTENDED LEARNING

1. Print and make copies of *The Jumping Jones Brothers Band* page and distribute to students. Display the Notebook page on the SMART Board. Explain that students will complete this page on their own, either in class or for homework. Remind them to apply what they have learned to solve this problem.

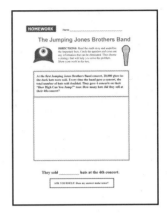

2. Review the problem at the beginning of the next class. Display the homework page on the SMART Board and invite volunteers to demonstrate how they solved the problem using the Five-Step Process. Then display the last page of the Notebook file to show one way of solving the problem.

Answer: 160,000 hats

The Fantastic
Five-Step Process

Directions: Use the Fantastic Five-Step Process to solve the problems below. Don't forget to show your thinking.

Go Frogs!

The Miami Frogs played their first four games this season on the road. Here's their schedule:

August 9	Smellbad Stadium	65,000 seats
August 12	Flytrap Pavilion	55,500 seats
August 19	Ratweed Coliseum	19,500 seats
August 27	Swamp Stump Park	60,000 seats

One of the games drew 61,000 fans. Where was it played?

Fast Flyers!

There are unusual birds on Planet Avian. Unusual, but fast! The Fling flies 206 miles per hour. The Flipple flies 210 miles per hour. The Flapper flies 406 miles per hour. The Flopper can't fly, but it can run at a pace of 214 miles per hour. One of these birds recently flew 412 miles in 2 hours. Which one was it?

THE SUPER 7 STRATEGIES

Once students are familiar with the Fantastic Five-Step Process, it's time to focus in on **Step #4: Choose a strategy and solve**. This particular step includes a wide range of choices, including some common problem-solving strategies that we call "The Super 7 Strategies." These strategies are:

#1:	Guess and Check
#2:	Draw a Picture
#3:	Make an Organized List
#4:	Look for a Pattern
#5:	Make a Table or Chart
#6:	Use Logical Reasoning
#7:	Work Backward

To help you teach each strategy, we provide simple word problems that you can use to model the strategy on the SMART Board. Students can then practice the strategy on their own with additional reproducible problems that you can assign as seatwork or as homework. All the word problems are on the CD, so you can work through them with the class after students have finished solving them independently.

We suggest introducing a new strategy every week or so. This way, students will have learned all of the Super 7 Strategies in two months. Learning and practicing these mathematical tools will make it easy for students to choose a strategy that fits a particular word problem and helps them arrive at a solution.

Guess and Check

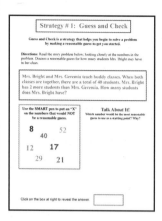

Sometimes the best way to tackle a difficult problem is to start with a reasonable guess.

GETTING READY

Before students arrive, have your SMART Board ready to go. Open the Guess and Check Notebook file. The first interactive page will appear on your SMART Board. If you wish, use the Screen Shade tool to conceal the page until you are ready to begin. Also open the Fantastic Five-Step Process Notebook file and go to the *Reviewing the Fantastic Five-Step Process* page.

INTRODUCING THE CONCEPT

1. Display *Reviewing the Fantastic Five-Step Process* on the SMART Board. Call on student volunteers to name the five steps. As they name the steps, click on the rectangles to reveal them in order.

2. Direct students' attention to **Step #4: Choose a strategy and solve**. Explain that over the next few weeks, they will be learning seven different strategies to help them solve word problems. They will find that certain strategies work very well with certain kinds of problems. Emphasize that they will continue to use the Fantastic Five-Step Process to analyze a problem, but when it comes to choosing a strategy, they will now have several options to choose from.

3. Display *Guess and Check* on the SMART Board. Tell students that the first strategy they will learn is called "Guess and Check." Explain this means to approach a problem with a reasonable guess to help get them started.

> Mrs. Bright and Mrs. Geremia teach buddy classes. When both classes are together, there are a total of 40 students. Mrs. Bright has 2 more students than Mrs. Geremia. How many students does Mrs. Bright have?

4. Call on a student volunteer to read aloud the problem on the board. Remind students to apply the Five-Step Process on this problem. Invite a volunteer to use the yellow highlighter to highlight the important facts in this problem. Then call on another student to highlight the question using the green highlighter. Direct students to look for key words and phrases, such as *total* or *more than*, that may help them make good choices about choosing an operation.

5. Next, have students look at the numbers in the problem and encourage them to apply their estimation skills. This is the key to making a "reasonable guess." Ask for a volunteer to guess how many students are in Mrs. Bright's class. After a first attempt at an answer, have the class consider whether the number is reasonable. Is it too high or too low? Would a higher number make more sense? Would a lower one? This is the "Check" part of Guess and Check.

6. Direct students' attention to the numbers inside the white box below the problem. Have them think about which numbers they could automatically cross out as unreasonable guesses. Invite a volunteer to come up and use the SMART pen to cross out an unreasonable guess. Ask the student to explain why he or she crossed out that number. *(For example, it can't be 40 because that's the total number of students in both classes.)*

TECH TIP

If students have trouble reaching the SMART toolbar when it's at the top of the screen, move it within reach. Click on the up-and-down arrow on the right end of your toolbar to move the toolbar to the bottom of your SMART Board. Click on the arrow again to return the toolbar to the top.

7. Discuss the "Talk About It" question: Which number would be the most reasonable guess to use as a starting point? Call on a student to choose a number from the white box and explain why he or she chose that number. To help students understand how the Guess and Check strategy works, think aloud through the steps of solving the problem using that number. For example, say the student chose 17. You might say, "So we're guessing that Mrs. Bright has 17 students. *(Use the SMART pen to write 17 on one side of the board.)* If that is true, and she has 2 more students than Mrs. Geremia, then *(write: 17 – 2 = 15)* that must mean that Mrs. Geremia has 15 students. Adding the students in both classes together *(15 + 17 = 32)*, we get 32, which is less than 40. So we know the number must be higher than 17. Let's try another one." Continue thinking aloud as you try another number.

8. To check the answer, click on the small red box at the bottom of the page. The box will fade out to reveal the correct answer. *(Mrs. Bright has 21 students.)*

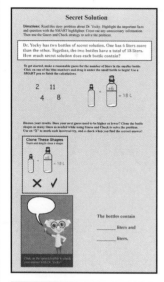

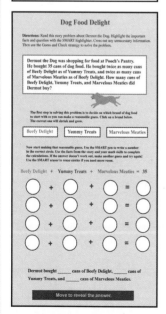

1. Display *Secret Solution* on the SMART Board. Use the Five-Step Process to examine this first problem together. Call on student volunteers to come to the board to highlight the important facts and the question. Have volunteers cross out information that can be eliminated.

> Dr. Yocky has two bottles of secret solution. One has 6 liters more than the other. Together, the two bottles have a total of 18 liters. How much secret solution does each bottle contain?

2. As with the previous problem, model this strategy by thinking aloud through the problem. You might say, "Let's start with a guess and say that the small bottle has 8 liters." (Drag the 8 on the left side to the smaller bottle.) Continue, "Since the other bottle has 6 liters more, then 8 + 6 = 14. So the larger bottle would have 14 liters. Added together that would be 22 liters. That's too high, so we should try a lower number."

3. Invite a student volunteer to come to the board and use the bottles to demonstrate his or her thinking. These bottles have been "infinitely cloned." That means every time the student touches or clicks on a bottle, it will make a new copy. The student can then drag that clone to the work space to help him or her solve the problem. If necessary, call on other volunteers as well, encouraging them to think aloud as they solve the problem.

4. Distribute photocopies of the *Guess and Check* worksheet (page 18) to students. Allow them to work in pairs, giving them ample time to solve the problems. Remind them to use the Five-Step Process and the Guess and Check strategy. When everyone has finished, display the *Space Adventure* Notebook page on the SMART Board. Invite students to come to the board to work through the steps and demonstrate their understanding. Repeat the process with the *Dog Food Delight* Notebook page.

Answers:

Secret Solution: 6 liters and 12 liters

Space Adventure: 5 grasshoppers and 5 starfish

Dog Food Delight: 10 cans of Beefy Delight, 5 cans of Yummy Treats, and 20 cans of Marvelous Meaties

EXTENDED LEARNING

1. Print and make copies of *The Centipede Sisters* page and distribute to students. Display the Notebook page on the SMART Board. Explain that students will complete this page on their own, either in class or for homework. Remind them to apply both the Five-Step Process and the Guess and Check strategy to solve this problem.

2. Review the problem at the beginning of the next class. Display the homework page on the SMART Board and invite volunteers to demonstrate how they solved the problem using the Guess and Check strategy. Then display the last page of the Notebook file to show one way of solving the problem.

Answer: Cindy is 65 millimeters long, and Cecilia is 35 millimeters long.

HOMEWORK   Name _____

The Centipede Sisters

DIRECTIONS: Read the math story and underline the important facts. Circle the question and cross out any information that can be eliminated. Then use the Guess and Check strategy to solve the problem.

Cindy Centipede and her sister Cecilia are both 11 years old. Together, they measure 100 millimeters long. Cindy is 30 millimeters longer than Cecilia. How long are the centipedes?

Cecilia is _____ millimeters long.
Cindy is _____ millimeters long.

ASK YOURSELF: Does my answer make sense?

Guess and Check

Directions: Use the Fantastic Five-Step Process and the Guess and Check strategy to solve the problems below. Don't forget to show your thinking.

Space Adventure

Space Commander Curious just completed a mission to Planet Peculiar, home to giant 6-legged grasshoppers and miniature 5-legged starfish. If Commander Curious saw 55 legs, how many grasshoppers and starfish did he see on the planet?

Dog Food Delight

Dermot the Dog was shopping for food at Pooch's Pantry. He bought 35 cans of dog food. He bought twice as many cans of Beefy Delight as of Yummy Treats, and twice as many cans of Marvelous Meaties as of Beefy Delight. How many cans of Beefy Delight, Yummy Treats, and Marvelous Meaties did Dermot buy?

Draw a Picture

When words get confusing, drawing the facts can sometimes help you get a clearer picture of what's being asked in a word problem.

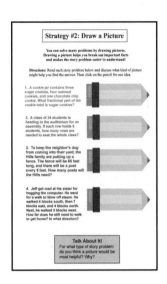

GETTING READY

Before students arrive, have your SMART Board ready to go. Open the Draw a Picture Notebook file. The first interactive page will appear on your SMART Board. If you wish, you may use the Screen Shade tool to conceal the page until you are ready to begin.

 INTRODUCING THE CONCEPT

1. Tell students: "When we worked with the Guess and Check strategy, we sometimes found it helpful to use a simple picture or diagram. Draw a Picture is a strategy we can use along with other strategies, such as Guess and Check, as well as on its own. This strategy helps us answer the first question in the Five-Step Process: What do we know?" Explain to students that in word problems, the facts can sometimes blend in with the text and get lost. By drawing the facts, you can arrange and manipulate them more easily and discover relationships more quickly.

2. Display *Draw a Picture* on the SMART Board. Slide down the Screen Shade to reveal the first problem. Call on a student volunteer to read aloud the problem. Then ask students: "What kind of picture might you draw to show the facts?" Listen to students' suggestions, then click on the pencil next to the problem to reveal one way to draw a picture. Tell students that drawings in problem solving should not be finished artwork. Rather encourage them to use simple symbols to represent elements in a word problem, such as a stick figure for people or a triangle for a tree.

3. Repeat with the other three problems, each time asking students for suggestions on how to draw the facts from the problem, then clicking on the pencil to reveal one way of representing them.

1. Display *Say Cheese!* on the SMART Board, using the Screen Shade to cover everything below the word problem. Use the Five-Step Process to examine the problem together. Call on volunteers to come to the board to highlight the important facts and the question. Have volunteers cross out information that can be eliminated.

> Charlie Cheese is making a birthday cake for his mom. He plans to decorate the cake with a circle of cheese cubes. Charlie has 7 cubes of cheddar cheese and would like to put 3 pieces of Swiss cheese between each pair of cheddar cubes. How many pieces of Swiss cheese does he need?

2. Next, ask: "What kind of picture might you draw to show the facts?" After students have offered their ideas, click or tap on the red button to remove the Screen Shade. Explain that the cake plate and symbols for both cheddar and Swiss cheese will help them with the drawing process. These symbols have been "infinitely cloned," so every time they touch or click on a symbol, it will make a new copy. They can drag each clone to the cake plate.

3. Invite a student volunteer to come to the board to show the facts. Ask: "Which type of cheese should we start with?" (*Cheddar*) Have the student clone and drag the cheddar cheese to the plate. "How many cubes of cheddar cheese do we need?" (*7*) Let the student repeat the clone-and-drag process until there are seven cheddar cubes around the plate. Remind him or her to leave space in between for the Swiss cheese.

4. Call on another volunteer to click and drag the Swiss cheese to the plate. Ask: "How many pieces of Swiss cheese should we put between each pair of cheddar cubes?" (*3*) Have the student clone and drag the Swiss cheese symbol and put three pieces between a pair of cheddar cubes. Have him or her repeat the process until the answer emerges. Ask: "How many pieces of Swiss cheese does Charlie need for his mom's cake?" (*21*)

5. Explain to students that if we tried to just visualize this problem, it would be much harder. Drawing the picture makes a clear representation of the facts that lead to an answer.

TECH TIP

If students have trouble dragging pictures across the board, demonstrate this process yourself. Sometimes it takes more than one try to get the picture ready to move. Explain to students that they should not take their finger off the SMART Board once they have touched the picture. The drag function works best when the student's finger stays in contact with the board.

6. Distribute photocopies of the *Draw a Picture* worksheet (page 23) to students. Allow students to work in pairs, giving them ample time to solve the problems. Remind them to use the Five-Step Process and the Draw a Picture strategy. When everyone has finished, display the *Keep Out!* Notebook page on the SMART Board. Invite students to come to the board to work through the steps and demonstrate their understanding. Repeat the process with the *Miss Drawitall's Desks* Notebook page.

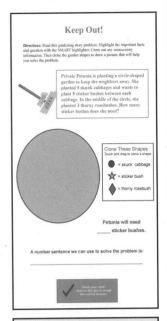

Answers:

Say Cheese! 21 pieces of Swiss cheese

Keep Out! 25 sticker bushes

Miss Drawitall's Desks: 22 children: 7 boys and 15 girls

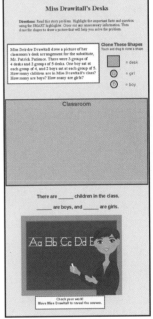

1. Print and make copies of the *Maxie's Famous Fish-Egg Omelet* page and distribute to students. Display the Notebook page on the SMART Board. Explain that students will complete this page on their own, either in class or for homework. Remind them to apply both the Five-Step Process and the Draw a Picture strategy to solve this problem.

2. Review the problem at the beginning of the next class. Display the homework page on the SMART Board and invite volunteers to demonstrate how they solved the problem using the Draw a Picture strategy. Then display the last page of the Notebook file to show one way of solving the problem.

Answer: 3 dozen fish eggs

Draw a Picture

Directions: Use the Fantastic Five-Step Process and the Draw a Picture strategy to solve the problems below. Don't forget to show your thinking.

Keep Out!

Private Petunia is planting a circle-shaped garden to keep the neighbors away. She planted 5 skunk cabbages and wants to plant 5 sticker bushes between each cabbage. In the middle of the circle, she planted 3 thorny rosebushes. How many sticker bushes does she need?

Miss Drawitall's Desks

Miss Deirdre Drawitall drew a picture of her classroom's desk arrangement for the substitute, Mr. Patrick Patience. There were 3 groups of 4 desks and 2 groups of 5 desks. One boy sat at each group of 4, and 2 boys sat at each group of 5. How many children are in Miss Drawitall's class? How many are boys? How many are girls?

Make an Organized List

Making a list is particularly useful in word problems that ask you to find all possible combinations. With a list, you can check and see if you've considered all the possibilities.

GETTING READY

Before students arrive, have your SMART Board ready to go. Open the Make an Organized List Notebook file. The first interactive page will appear on your SMART Board. If you wish, use the Screen Shade tool to conceal the page until you are ready to begin.

 INTRODUCING THE CONCEPT

> **TECH TIP**
>
> If students have trouble writing with the SMART pens, check that they are holding the stylus correctly. If a student's wrist or hand rubs against the screen while writing, his or her writing will appear garbled and illegible. When using these pens, only the stylus tip should make contact with the SMART Board. If the writing is not showing up on the screen, try pushing a little harder with the SMART pen. Applying pressure with the pens will not damage the SMART Board.

1. Display *Make an Organized List* on the SMART Board. Explain that this strategy helps us identify and organize important information from a word problem. Making a list of the data or facts can help us see patterns and relationships that may exist. This strategy is particularly helpful for problems in which combinations must be determined. Listing all possible combinations is essential to finding the solution.

> Oliver wants to buy an eraser for 25 cents. He has I quarter, 2 dimes, 2 nickels, and 5 pennies in his pocket. How many different ways can Oliver make 25 cents?

2. Call on a student volunteer to read aloud the problem on the page. Invite a student volunteer to come up to the board and use a SMART pen to write one possible combination. Ask students if they can see other ways to make 25 cents from the coins Oliver has. Call on various volunteers to list other possible combinations. Then click on the yellow paper to reveal all possible combinations. From the list, we determine that there are four possible ways Oliver can make 25 cents.

3. Explain to students that when making a list, they don't have to write the full name of an element in a problem. Abbreviations, like D for dime, work just fine.

1. Display *Traveling Teams* on the SMART Board. Use the Five-Step Process to examine this problem together. Call on volunteers to come to the board to highlight the important facts and the question. Have volunteers cross out unnecessary information.

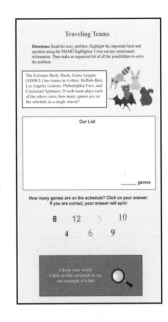

> The Extreme Duck, Duck, Goose League (XDDGL) has teams in 4 cities: Buffalo Bats, Los Angeles Lichens, Philadelphia Furs, and Cincinnati Spinners. If each team plays each of the others once, how many games are on the schedule in a single season?

2. Before starting a list, remind students that they can abbreviate the names of the various elements in a problem. For example, BB could represent the team Buffalo Bats. You might also suggest that they include a key with the abbreviations to help them remember what each one stands for.

3. Explain that a good way to start is to take one team and list the games it will play against each of the other teams. For example, take the Buffalo Bats (BB):

    BB vs. LL

    BB vs. PF

    BB vs. CS

    Next, take another team, like the Los Angeles Lichens (LL), and list its possible games. Remind students that they don't need to repeat this team's game against the Buffalo Bats, because it's already listed above.

    LL vs. PF

    LL vs. CS

    Continue with the Philadelphia Furs (PF), again keeping in mind that its games against the Buffalo Bats and the Los Angeles Lichens are already listed above. What's left?

    PF vs. CS

4. Ask students: "Do we need to list the games for the Cincinnati Spinners (CS)? Why or why not?" (*No, because the team's games against BB, LL, and PF are already in the list above.*) From this list, we can see that six games would be scheduled in a single season. Explain to students that organizing a list this way helps them easily compare the combinations of teams so they can make sure they are not missing any or repeating any.

5. Distribute photocopies of the *Make an Organized List* worksheet (page 28) to students. Allow students to work in pairs, giving them ample time to solve the problems. Remind them to use the Five-Step Process and the Make an Organized List strategy. When everyone has finished, display the *Tasty Treats* Notebook page on the SMART Board. Invite students to come to the board to work through the steps and demonstrate their understanding. Repeat the process with the *Only the Finest!* Notebook page.

Answers:

Traveling Teams: 6 games

Tasty Treats: 6 ways

Only the Finest! 3 combinations

EXTENDED LEARNING

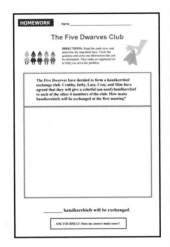

1. Print and make copies of *The Five Dwarves Club* page and distribute to students. Display the Notebook page on the SMART Board. Explain that students will complete this page on their own, either in class or for homework. Remind them to apply both the Five-Step Process and the Make an Organized List strategy to solve this problem.

2. Review the problem at the beginning of the next class. Display the homework page on the SMART Board and invite volunteers to demonstrate how they solved the problem using the Make an Organized List strategy. Then display the last page of the Notebook file to show one way of solving the problem.

Answer: 20 handkerchiefs will be exchanged at the first meeting.

Make an Organized List

Directions: Use the Fantastic Five-Step Process and the Make an Organized List strategy to solve the problems below. Don't forget to show your thinking.

Tasty Treats

Healthy Helga has 19 cents. She earned it by baby-sitting for her neighbor's pet Pomeranian, Pickles. Helga has decided to spend it all on tasty treats. She can buy broccoli florets for 10 cents, stale peanuts for 5 cents, and mustard drops for a penny. How many different ways can Helga spend her money?

Only the Finest!

Countess Caroline Cardinal is a very snobby bird. She demands only the finest imported sparkling water to fill her birdbath. Her birdbath holds 10 liters of water. The water is sold in 4-liter and 1-liter bottles. How many combinations of 4- and 1-liter bottles can she buy to fill her birdbath? (While fussy, the countess isn't wasteful. She uses all the water in the bottles for her birdbath.)

Look for a Pattern

Some problems have hidden patterns that, if found, offer clues to the solution. Look for relationships between the numbers in a problem to get started.

GETTING READY

Before students arrive, have your SMART Board ready to go. Open the Look for a Pattern Notebook file. The first interactive page will appear on your SMART Board. Use the Screen Shade tool to conceal the page until you are ready to begin.

 INTRODUCING THE CONCEPT

1. Explain to students that making lists and drawing pictures may reveal patterns that exist within the facts of a problem. When looking for a pattern, have students ask themselves: "Is there a relationship between the numbers in the problem? How far apart are they from one another? Do they increase or decrease by certain amounts in certain ways?" Tell students that asking these questions often leads to a good solution.

2. Display *Look for a Pattern* on the SMART Board. Use the Five-Step Process to examine this problem together. Call on student volunteers to come to the board and highlight the important facts and the question. Have volunteers cross out information that can be eliminated.

> Sarah is selling her famous sardine pies. On Monday, she sold 1 pie; on Tuesday, she sold 2 pies; on Wednesday, she sold 4; and on Thursday, she sold 7. If the pattern continues, how many pies will she sell on Friday?

3. Explain to students that in using this strategy, it is important to organize the information in a way so a pattern can become apparent. Invite a student volunteer to list the number of pies Sarah sells each day. Then guide the class to examine the relationship between the numbers. You might say: "We can see that the numbers are increasing, but by how much are they increasing each time?" Look at the first two numbers and point out that 2 is 1 more than 1:

Then look at the next number and its relationship to the previous number:

Finally, look at the last given number. Ask, "How is 7 related to 4?" (*7 is 3 more than 4*)

$$4 \nearrow + 3$$
$$7$$

Ask students, "If the pattern continues, by how much do you think will the next number increase?" (*By 4*) So, adding 4 to 7, we can tell that Sarah will sell 11 pies on Friday. Point out how listing and analyzing the information this way helped us find the pattern more easily.

1. Display *Trendy Trudy* on the SMART Board. Use the Five-Step Process to examine the problem together. Call on student volunteers to come to the board and highlight the important facts and the question and to cross out information that can be eliminated.

> Trendy Trudy bought a necklace from the famous designer, Desmond Diamond. Hanging from the necklace are jewels shaped like triangles, hexagons, and pentagons. The jewels follow a pattern: triangle, hexagon, pentagon. If the pattern continues, how many sides will the 30th jewel have?

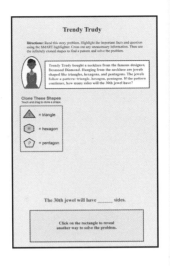

2. Guide students to notice that this problem already gives the pattern to follow. Ask, "What is the pattern?" (*triangle, hexagon, pentagon*) Explain to students that one way to find out how many sides the 30th jewel has is by drawing the shapes following the pattern until they reach the 30th jewel. Invite a student to come up to the SMART Board and use the infinitely cloned shapes to continue the pattern. Using this strategy (Draw a Picture), students will see that the 30th jewel is a pentagon and thus has 5 sides.

💡 **TECH TIP**

Did you goof up? Don't worry! Notebook offers a backtracking tool to let you click back to before it all happened! Simply click on the blue reverse arrow ↺ to undo your last action. You may repeat to undo several actions. And if you change your mind, just click the forward arrow ↻ to redo the action.

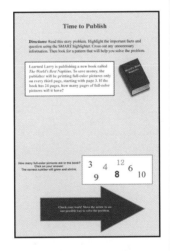

3. Ask students, "Can you think of another way to get to the answer much more quickly?" Entertain a few answers, then click on the rectangular box at the bottom of the page to reveal another way of finding the solution.

4. Distribute photocopies of the *Look for a Pattern* worksheet (page 33) to students. Allow students to work in pairs, giving them ample time to solve the problems. Remind them to use the Five-Step Process and the Look for a Pattern strategy. When everyone has finished, display the *Time to Publish* Notebook page on the SMART Board. Invite students to come to the board to work through the steps and demonstrate their understanding. Repeat the process with the *Stagehand Steve* Notebook page.

Answers:

Trendy Trudy: 5 sides

Time to Publish: 8 pages

Stagehand Steve: 32 chairs

1. Print and make copies of the *Ricky Weighs In* page and distribute to students. Display the Notebook page on the SMART Board. Explain that students will complete this page on their own, either in class or for homework. Remind them to apply both the Five-Step Process and the Look for a Pattern strategy to solve this problem.

2. Review the problem at the beginning of the next class. Display the homework page on the SMART Board and invite volunteers to demonstrate how they solved the problem using the Look for a Pattern strategy. Then display the last page of the Notebook file to show one way of solving the problem.

Answer: 32 kilograms

Look for a Pattern

Directions: Use the Fantastic Five-Step Process and the Look for a Pattern strategy to solve the problems below. Don't forget to show your thinking.

Time to Publish

Learned Larry is publishing a new book called *The World's Best Napkins*. To save money, the publisher will be printing full-color pictures only on every third page, starting with page 3. If the book has 24 pages, how many pages of full-color pictures will it have?

Stagehand Steve

Steve the Stagehand is setting up chairs for the school orchestra's next concert. He put 4 chairs in the first row, 8 chairs in the second row, 12 chairs in the third row, and so on. If he continues with this pattern, how many chairs will he put in the eighth row?

Make a Table or Chart

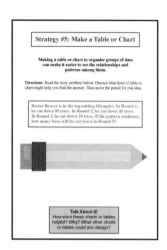

Organizing data in tables and charts often reveals the relationship between two sets of numbers, making patterns more apparent.

GETTING READY

Before students arrive, have your SMART Board ready to go. Open the Make a Table or Chart Notebook file. The first interactive page will appear on your SMART Board. Use the Screen Shade tool to conceal the page until you are ready to begin.

INTRODUCING THE CONCEPT

1. Do a quick review of the strategy Make an Organized List. Explain to students that making a list is helpful when dealing with a simple set of facts. However, some problems present more complex sets of data, and the best way to organize them is to create a table or chart. This helps them see the relationships between the sets, and patterns become more apparent.

> Buster Beaver is in the log-cutting Olympics. In Round 1, he cut down 80 trees. In Round 2, he cut down 40 trees. In Round 3, he cut down 20 trees. If the pattern continues, how many trees will he cut down in Round 5?

2. Display *Make a Table or Chart* on the SMART Board. Call on a student to read the problem aloud. Have students suggest ways they might organize the facts of the problem. Then drag the pencil to one side to reveal a table with the given information. Ask students, "Do you see some kind of pattern from these numbers?" (*In every round, the number of trees Buster cuts is halved.*) "How many trees will he cut down in Round 5?" (5)

3. Discuss with students how the table helped them organize the information so they could see a pattern more readily. They could then easily extend the pattern to get to the answer. Caution students as to how far to extend the data. For example, there's no reason to go beyond Round 5 because that would be more information than they need to answer the question.

1. Display *Bone Appétit!* on the SMART Board, using the Screen Shade to cover the table below the word problem. Use the Five-Step Process to examine this problem together. Call on student volunteers to come to the board to highlight the important facts and the question. Have volunteers cross out information that can be eliminated.

> Claude, the Canine Chef, has created a new dish for his fellow pooches: dog-food lasagna. The lasagna can be bought in boxes with a single serving or in packages with 5 servings. Each serving weighs 5 ounces. If you wanted to buy exactly 23 servings, how many ways could you do it?

2. Ask students, "How might we organize the data?" Explain that while one way is to make a list, given that there are two sets of data to keep track of, making a table offers a neater option for recording all the possibilities. Remove the Screen Shade to reveal the table with two columns. Point out the heading on each column—5-serving package and 1-serving box—and the first row under the heading. Explain that one way to make 23 servings is to buy four 5-serving packages and three 1-serving boxes. Challenge students to think of other possible combinations and call on volunteers to come to the board to add more rows and list other combinations. Finally, invite a student volunteer to use the SMART eraser to reveal the answer at the bottom of the page.

TECH TIP

Whenever you use the SMART eraser, be sure to put it back in its spot when you are done. If you do not replace the eraser, the SMART Board will continue reading your next action as an erasure.

3. Distribute photocopies of the *Make a Table or Chart* worksheet (page 37) to students. Allow students to work in pairs, giving them ample time to solve the problems. Remind them to use the Five-Step Process and the Make a Table or Chart strategy. When everyone has finished, display the *Watch Out!* Notebook page on the SMART Board. Invite students to come to the board to work through the steps and demonstrate their understanding. Repeat the process with the *Rock On!* Notebook page.

Answers:

Bone Appétit! 5 ways

Watch Out! 50 meters

Rock On! 10:15 p.m.

1. Print and make copies of the *Healthy Brownies* page and distribute to students. Display the Notebook page on the SMART Board. Explain that students will complete this page on their own, either in class or for homework. Remind them to apply both the Five-Step Process and the Make a Table or Chart strategy to solve this problem.

2. Review the problem at the beginning of the next class. Display the homework page on the SMART Board and invite volunteers to demonstrate how they solved the problem using the Make a Table or Chart strategy. Point out that the problem already has part of the information in a table and all they needed to do was look for a pattern emerging from the table. How do the numbers in the top of the chart relate to the numbers in the bottom part of the chart? Then go to the last page of the Notebook file to show one way of solving the problem.

Answer: 5 packages

Make a Table or Chart

Directions: Use the Fantastic Five-Step Process and Make a Table or Chart strategy to solve the problems below. Don't forget to show your thinking.

Watch Out!

Science enthusiast Lucinda enjoys making things bounce, so she decided to conduct a fun experiment. She dropped her father's expensive new watch from the roof of her building, which is 800 meters high. After the watch hit the pavement the first time, it bounced up 400 meters. After the second bounce, it rose 200 meters. If the pattern continues, how high will the watch rise on the fourth bounce?

Rock On!

Everyone's favorite band, The Wild Watermelons, will be playing at Silly Sid's Stadium all weekend. On Friday night, the band will play 3 shows. Each show lasts for 45 minutes, followed by a 30-minute break. If the band starts playing at 7:00 p.m., when will they finish?

SMART Board Lessons: Math Word Problems © 2010 by Bob Krech, Scholastic Teaching Resources

Use Logical Reasoning

Strategy #6: Use Logical Reasoning

Logical reasoning problems often contain many facts that need to be organized and analyzed. Strategies we have already learned—such as drawing pictures, making lists, tables, and charts, and looking for patterns—come in very handy. Using a logic matrix or a Venn diagram can also help.

Directions: Read the story problem below. Highlight the important facts and question using the SMART highlighter. Cross out any information that can be eliminated. Then use the Logic Matrix below to organize your information. Clone the ✓ to mark the facts that are false. Clone the ✗ to mark the facts that are true. This will help you determine in an organized way what spell-cast on whom.

William, the Wizard-in-Training, cast 4 different spells on 4 classmates, but now he can't remember which spell was cast on whom. These are the facts he remembers: Romulus was not turned into pudding; Julius was shrunk to the size of a gerbil; Virgil neither glowed in the dark nor developed an intense appetite for applesauce; Clem did not glow in the dark. Which spell was cast on Clem?

Logic Matrix

	Romulus	Julius	Virgil	Clem
Pudding				
Gerbil				
Glow				
Applesauce				

Clone These Shapes
Touch and drag to clone a shape.   ✓   ✗

Which spell was cast on Clem?

Some word problems require students to use deductive reasoning to get to the solution. These problems often present several facts that are best organized—and analyzed—using a logic matrix or a Venn diagram.

GETTING READY

Before students arrive, have your SMART Board ready to go. Open the Use Logical Reasoning Notebook file. The first interactive page will appear on your SMART Board. If you wish, use the Screen Shade tool to conceal the page until you are ready to begin.

 INTRODUCING THE CONCEPT

1. Review the different strategies students have learned so far that involve making sense of information, such as Make an Organized List and Make a Table or Chart. Explain that the key to this next strategy, Use Logical Reasoning, is also organizing and analyzing information. Logic problems often include several facts that can be challenging to keep track of. Drawing pictures and making lists, tables, and charts help, but the most useful tools for logic-type problems are a logic matrix and a Venn diagram.

> William, the Wizard-in-Training, cast 4 different spells on 4 classmates, but now he can't remember which spell was cast on whom. These are the facts he remembers: Romulus was not turned into pudding; Julius was shrunk to the size of a gerbil; Virgil neither glowed in the dark nor developed an intense appetite for applesauce; Clem did not glow in the dark. Which spell was cast on Clem?

2. Display *Use Logical Reasoning* on the SMART Board. Call on a student to read the problem aloud. Students are sure to notice that there's a lot of information to sort through in this problem. Explain that this type of problem is best solved using a logic matrix. A logic matrix helps us organize facts so we can gradually eliminate all the different possibilities until only one remains, which must be the answer.

3. Guide students to observe how the matrix below the problem has been set up: It's a 4 x 4 grid, because four spells were cast on four classmates. Across the top of the grid are the classmates' names, and along the left side are the spells that have been cast. Below the grid are infinite clones of a checkmark (√) and an X to help analyze the information.

4. Refer students back to the problem to get the facts. The first fact says that Romulus was not turned into pudding. Thinking aloud, point to the column with Romulus's name on top and move your finger down next to the spell that says Pudding. Explain, "We can X this box out, because we know that Romulus was not turned to pudding." Demonstrate how to click and drag the X to clone and move it to the box.

5. Invite a student volunteer to tackle the next clue: Julius was shrunk to the size of a gerbil. Ask: "Which mark would you use and where would you put it?" (*The √ in the box where Julius and Gerbil intersect*) Ask students, "Would any of the other students have been shrunk to the size of a gerbil as well?" (*No*) Have the student clone and drag the X to the other boxes in the gerbil row. Explain that this helps narrow down the information.

6. Continue calling on students to fill out the rest of the logic matrix based on the facts of the problem. When the entire logic matrix has been filled, students will see that Clem developed an intense appetite for applesauce. Click on the wizard at the bottom of the page to confirm the answer.

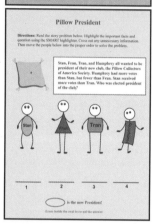

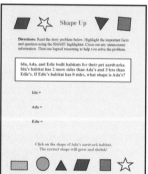

1. Display *Thankful* on the SMART Board, using the Screen Shade to cover everything below the word problem. Use the Five-Step Process to examine this problem together. Call on student volunteers to come to the board to highlight the important facts and the question. Have volunteers cross out information that can be eliminated.

> The Happy Henswangle family had a big Thanksgiving dinner. There was a choice of main courses: turkey, ham, or both. Seven of the family members had turkey on their plates. Seven had ham on their plates. Since there are 10 Henswangles, how many had both turkey and ham?

2. Explain to students that in problems such as this, in which two sets of information are being compared, a Venn diagram—two overlapping circles— can be a useful tool for organizing information. Remove the Screen Shade to reveal the Venn diagram. Invite a student volunteer to drag the infinitely cloned turkey to where it belongs on the Venn diagram. Ask, "How many turkeys should we put in the circle labeled 'Turkey'?" (7) Have another student do the same for the ham.

3. Now here comes the tricky part: There are only 10 Henswangles, but the Venn diagram will have a total of 14 plates of turkey and ham. Obviously some of the Henswangles had both turkey and ham. The question is, how many of them did? Challenge students to think about how they might use the Venn diagram and the cloned shapes to figure out the answer. (*One way is to delete a turkey and a ham from each circle and replace them with a B in the overlapping part labeled "Both." That would represent a plate with both turkey and ham. Continue until there are only 10 plates left in the diagram.*)

4. Distribute photocopies of the *Use Logical Reasoning* worksheet (page 42) to students. Allow students to work in pairs, giving them ample time to solve the problems. Remind them to use the Five-Step Process and the Use Logical Reasoning strategy. When everyone has finished, display the *Pillow President* Notebook page on the SMART Board. Invite students to come to the board to work through the steps and demonstrate their understanding. Repeat the process with the *Shape Up* Notebook page.

Answers:

Thankful: 4 Henswangles had both turkey and ham.

Pillow President: Fran

Shape Up: Triangle

TECH TIP

To delete an unwanted object on a Notebook page, select it by clicking on it with your finger. Check that a blue dotted line surrounds the selected object. Then touch the red X in your toolbar.

EXTENDED LEARNING

1. Print and make copies of the *Roscoe's Termite Ranch* page and distribute to students. Display the *Roscoe's Termite Ranch* Notebook page on the SMART Board. Explain that students will complete this page on their own, either in class or for homework. Remind them to apply both the Five-Step Process and the Use Logical Reasoning strategy to solve this problem.

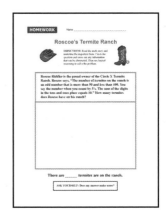

2. Review the problem at the beginning of the next class. Display the homework page on the SMART Board and invite volunteers to demonstrate how they solved the problem using the Use Logical Reasoning strategy. Then display the last page of the Notebook file to show one way of solving the problem.

Answer: 55 termites

Use Logical Reasoning

Directions: Use the Fantastic Five-Step Process and the Use Logical Reasoning strategy to solve the problems below. Don't forget to show your thinking.

Pillow President

Stan, Fran, Tran, and Humphrey all wanted to be president of their new club, the Pillow Collectors of America Society. Humphrey had more votes than Stan, but fewer than Fran. Stan received more votes than Tran. Who was elected president of the club?

Shape Up

Ida, Ada, and Edie built habitats for their pet aardvarks. Ida's habitat has 2 more sides than Ada's and 3 less than Edie's. If Edie's habitat has 8 sides, what shape is Ada's?

Work Backward

Working backward is the best strategy to use when you know how a problem ends up but need to figure out how it started. The trick is knowing where to begin and how to use inverse operations.

GETTING READY

Before students arrive, have your SMART Board ready to go. Open the Work Backward Notebook file. The first interactive page will appear on your SMART Board. If you wish, use the Screen Shade tool to conceal the page until you are ready to begin.

INTRODUCING THE CONCEPT

1. Tell students that they will now learn another problem-solving strategy called Work Backward. This strategy is particularly useful when we know how a problem ends up, but we don't know how it started. Explain that in this type of problem, we're usually looking for an unknown value. Using a letter or symbol to represent this unknown can be helpful.

> Daphne and Desdimona played together for 3 hours. They played Catch the Wasp for an hour and 15 minutes, juggled mangoes for an hour, and wrestled pigs for the rest of the time. How much time did they spend wrestling pigs?

2. Display *Work Backward* on the SMART Board. Call on a student volunteer to read the problem aloud. Explain to students that when dealing with this type of problem, it's important to know where to begin and how to use *inverse operations*. Thinking aloud as you solve the problem on the board will help students understand your thought process. You might say, for example, "We know that Daphne and Desdimona played together for 3 hours, so that's the total time (or TT). We also know that they did three things in those 3 hours: they played Catch the Wasp (CW), juggled mangoes (JM), and wrestled pigs (WP). If we were to write that in an equation, it would be

$$TT = CW + JM + WP$$

We have to find our way back to see how much of that time was spent wrestling pigs. First, we know they played Catch the Wasp for 1 hour and 15 minutes.

3 hrs = 1 hr 15 min + JM + WP

So let's subtract 1 hour and 15 minutes from 3 hours.

3 hrs − 1 hr 15 min = 1 hr 45 min = JM + WP

That leaves us with 1 hour and 45 minutes, during which they juggled mangoes and wrestled pigs. We know they juggled mangoes for one hour, so

1 hr 45 min = 1 hr + WP

If we subtract that from the last time, we're left with 45 minutes.

1 hr 45 min − 1 hr = 45 min = WP

So they must have wrestled pigs for 45 minutes."

3. Click on the pig at the bottom of the page to reveal the correct answer.

 TECH TIP

When using these Notebook activities, it's easy to find a spot to record and display ideas or equations. Just scroll down to the bottom of the page and click on Extend Page. Use the extra white space to record your notes. This is a perfect way to record students' thinking.

INTERACTIVE LEARNING

1. Display *Money Matters* on the SMART Board. Use the Fantastic Five-Step Process to examine this problem together. Call on student volunteers to come to the board to highlight the important facts and the question. Have volunteers cross out information that can be eliminated.

> Carla went to the store and bought a book for $2.67. The clerk gave her back $2.35 change. How much money did Carla give the clerk to begin with?

2. Ask students, "What information are we looking for? (*How much money Carla gave to the clerk*) What information do we have? (*The book costs $2.67, and Carla got $2.35 in change.*) How can we use the information we have to get to the answer we need?"

3. Call on a student volunteer to come to the SMART Board and, using the Work Backward strategy, talk through the process of solving the problem. Then click on the dollar bill at the bottom to reveal the solution.

4. Distribute photocopies of the *Work Backward* worksheet (page 47) to students. Allow students to work in pairs, giving them ample time to solve the problems. Remind them to use the Five-Step Process and the Work Backward strategy. When everyone has finished, display the *Super Sales* Notebook page on the SMART Board. Invite students to come to the board to work through the steps and demonstrate their understanding. Repeat the process with the *Waldo Worm* Notebook page.

Answers:

Money Matters: $5.02

Super Sales: 400 CDs arrived on Thursday.

Waldo Worm: Each of the remaining sides is 7 inches long.

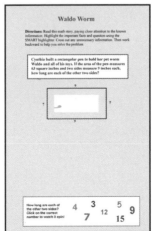

1. Print and make copies of the *Fishy Frosting* page and distribute to students. Display the Notebook page on the SMART Board. Explain that students will complete this page on their own, either in class or for homework. Remind them to apply the Five-Step Process and the Work Backward strategy to solve this problem.

2. Review the problem at the beginning of the next class. Display the homework page on the SMART Board and invite volunteers to demonstrate how they solved the problem using the Work Backward strategy. Then display the last page of the Notebook file to show one way of solving the problem.

Answer: 12 pounds of anchovies

Work Backward

Directions: Use the Fantastic Five-Step Process and the Work Backward strategy to solve the problems below. Don't forget to show your thinking.

Super Sales

Maestro Melvin's Music Store has been selling lots of copies of the new hit CD *I Love Cheese* by The Marvelous Mouse Band. On Thursday, the first shipment of CDs arrived. On Friday, Melvin sold 90 copies. On Saturday, he sold 130. On Sunday, he sold 60 copies and had 120 left at the end of the day. How many CDs arrived on Thursday?

Waldo Worm

Cynthia built a rectangular pen to hold her pet worm Waldo and all of his toys. If the area of the pen measures 63 square inches and two sides measure 9 inches each, how long are each of the other two sides?

Wrapping Up

By now, students will have had several opportunities to practice all Super 7 Strategies as well as the Fantastic Five-Step Process. Remind students that certain strategies work better for some problems and that sometimes more than one strategy can be used in conjunction with another.

For more practice, print and make copies of the *Review Sheet* Notebook page and distribute to students. Use these problems to continue this unit of study or to review the problem-solving processes and strategies. You might take five to ten minutes a week at the beginning of a math class to do a word problem together, discuss it, and share a few strategies. As students work on the problems, encourage them to "show their thinking" by writing out their solution process. This will help keep the problem-solving strategies fresh in students' minds over the next few weeks. Also, seeing their thought process will help you assess where they might still need extra help.

With these new problem-solving tools, students will be more than ready to take on any mathematical word problems, and more important, any math problems they encounter in their own lives.

Answers to Review Sheet:

1. Basil found 5 slugs in the smaller bag.

2. $1,500

3. Belinda Bright

4. The two uniform numbers are 12 and 14.

5. The monument has 36 concrete pizzas on it.